Rabbit Ravioli

Photographs, Recipes &
Literary Vignettes of Newfoundland

Kitty Drake & Ned Pratt

BREAKWATER

BREAKWATER
100 Water Street
P.O. Box 2188
St. John's, NF
A1E 6E6

Design by Susan Wright

Canadian Cataloguing in Publication Data
Drake, Kitty, 1946-

Rabbit ravioli

Includes bibliographical references and index.
ISBN 1-55081-094-4

1. Cookery, Canadian – Newfoundland style.
2. Cookery – Newfoundland. 3. Newfoundland –
Pictorial works. I. Pratt, Ned, 1964- II. Title.

TX715.6.D72 1994 641.59718 C94-950217-0

Text copyright © 1994 Kitty Drake
Photos copyright © 1994 Ned Pratt
Design copyright © 1994 Breakwater

Printed in Hong Kong by Wing King Tong Co. Ltd.

Rabbit Ravioli

Anne & Alan

A wonderful little book that has refreshing
recipes and photographs. I have had a copy for a few
now. I enjoy cooking from it. Also makes a nice
coffee table (tea if you care) book.

Merry Christmas 1995

Love Steve & Karen

"As soon as the Sun makes its appearance the cold is
dissipat'd and its luminous rays are gratefull and pleasing.
This time of the year is call'd Spring – in Newfoundland."

– Aaron Thomas, Able Seaman, 1794

Acknowledgements

I wish to thank my friend Philip Pratt and sister Becky Boger for their patience and support. I would also like to thank Eric Facey who lent me his library of Newfoundland literature, fed me, and provided the inspiration behind many of the quotes.

For allowing me to ransack their homes for props, I wish to thank Debbie Powers, Mary Pratt, Bill Donnelly, Lois Dinn, and Christine Pratt.

I also wish to thank the people of Notre Dame Bay, in particular Gus and Ruby Jefferies of Exploits who introduced me to the best of Newfoundland.

- Kitty Drake

For their support and encouragement, I would like to thank my wife Sheila, my parents Christopher and Mary Pratt, and my former employer Michael Harris.

I also wish to acknowledge the people and the place of St. Mary's Bay where I grew up and learned to look at Newfoundland.

- Ned Pratt

Marine synopsis for Newfoundland issued by the
Newfoundland Weather Centre of Environment Canada at Gander,
3:00 AM NST Wednesday 23 February 1994

A low pressure system lying east of forecast waters will intensify today
and then move eastward on Thursday. Moderate to strong northerlies over
most waters are forecast to increase to gale to storm force as the low intensifies....
Marine interests are advised that storm warnings are continued for the
Belle Isle Bank and the Funk Island Bank. Freezing spray warnings
are continued for the southwest coast south coast Belle Isle Bank Funk Island
Bank and the southeastern and southwestern Grand Banks.

- The Newfoundland Weather Centre of Environment Canada at Gander, 23 February 1994

Contents

Contents

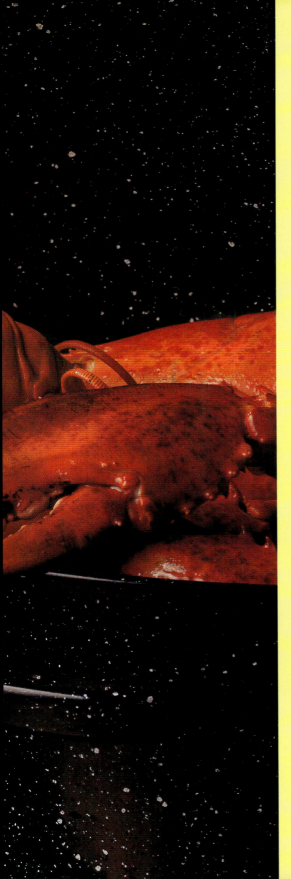

Seafood

"I consol'd myself under the
Idea of having a good Supper
of Lobsters, but on making
enquiry I found that there was
neither Oil nor Vinegar in
Portugal Cove. Without one
or the other this Fish,
in my opinion,
is not worth eating."

- Aaron Thomas, Able Seaman, 1794

"In all my long life, fishing always, I never sold a fish for money before...."

- George Francis Durgin, 1908
"I Never Sold a Fish for Money Before"

Scallops with Roasted Red Pepper Sauce

This rich, creamy, slightly tangy sauce accents the sweet delicate flavor of scallops.
It goes equally well with any mild white fish, such as halibut, monk fish or cod.
Serves 6 - 8.

Roasted Red Pepper Purée

6 red peppers
1.2 - 2.5 ml (1/4 - 1/2 tsp.)
 red pepper flakes
62 ml (1/4 cup) unsalted butter
30 ml (2 tbsp.) sugar
30 ml (2 tbsp.) vinegar

Place red peppers on cookie sheet and roast in 450°F oven until blackened. Remove from oven and immediately cover with a cloth until cool. This allows them to sweat which loosens the skins. Peel and discard the seeds. Chop them coarsely.

Melt butter in pan. Add peppers, pepper flakes, sugar, and vinegar. Cook over low heat, stirring occasionally until dry. Purée in food processor and press through sieve.

This purée keeps well in the refrigerator or freezer.

Roasted Red Pepper Sauce for Seafood

250 ml (1 cup) red pepper purée
62 ml (1/4 cup) unsalted butter
500 ml (2 cups) dry white wine
125 ml (1/2 cup) medium sherry
500 ml (2 cups) cream
Beurre manie
Salt and pepper
1 - 2 kg (2 - 4 lbs.) scallops
500 g (1/2 lb.) pasta (spinach or
  black pepper and basil linguini
  or fettuccine is particularly nice)

Place wine and sherry in a saucepan. Bring to a boil and boil until reduced to a syrup. Whisk in the cream and boil until reduced by 1/2. Thicken with beurre manie, if needed, until it is the consistency of heavy whipping cream. Whisk in red pepper purée. Taste for salt and pepper.

Sauté the scallops in butter. Stir in the sauce. Serve over pasta.

Langosta Manolo

This recipe comes from our Cuban friends who prepare it with their favoured clawless Carribean lobster. No matter which you consider best, it is an unusual and delicious way to enjoy lobster. Serves 4.

4 live lobsters, 500 g (1 1/4 lbs.) each
Olive oil
1 red pepper, coarsely chopped
6 large garlic cloves, coarsely chopped
1 medium onion, coarsely chopped
100 ml (4 oz.) tomato paste
1 bottle beer
Juice of 1/2 lemon
62 ml (1/4 cup) soya sauce
Salt

To prepare the lobster, immerse momentarily in boiling water, then separate the tail and claws from the body, which kills it instantly. Pull the top shell from the body and discard the old woman (a lump of bitter black stuff up near the head) and the liver. Cut the tail in segments at each joint. Crack the claws.

Sauté the red pepper, garlic, and onion in the olive oil until tender. Add the beer, soya sauce, tomato paste and salt. Bring to a boil and add the lobster. Cover and steam the lobster 10 minutes or until red, turning once.

Serve hot with white rice and black beans.

"She's made from wood, but she's no ordinary boat, Sir,
Cut in the fall and seasoned 'til midwinter's over.
See the high round bow and she's all tucked under,
And from stem to stern she's our Newfoundland wonder."

– Kevin Blackmore and Ray Johnson
"Makin' for the Harbour"

Caribbean Crab Backs

Newfoundland has had a long friendly relationship with the Caribbean Islands, trading salt cod for molasses, sugar and rum. While salt cod is considered a delicacy on the Islands, crab, on the other hand, is a snack, eaten like popcorn as one walks the streets.
Makes 8 appetizers or 4 main courses.

500 g (1 lb.) crab meat, fresh or frozen
30 ml (2 tbsp.) onions, finely minced
30 ml (2 tbsp.) red pepper, finely minced
30 ml (2 tbsp.) hot pepper, finely minced
1 clove garlic, finely minced
250 ml (1 cup) dry bread crumbs
15 ml (1 tbsp.) parsley, finely chopped
1 egg, slightly beaten
Juice of 1/2 lemon
Dash of Carribean style hot sauce
62 ml (1/4 cup) cream

To make the filling, thoroughly mix together all the ingredients. Lightly oil the insides of the crab backs. Fill with the crab mixture. Bake 350°F for 20 minutes.

Serve with hot sauce, tart chutney or relish.

"Having no reason for my scheme
Beyond the logic of a Dream."

- E.J. Pratt
"The Depression Ends"

Scallops, Mussels & Spinach
in Creamy White Wine Sauce

Wild mussels are tastier than cultivated ones but have the disadvantage of often
being full of pearls. Either kind is delicious in this rich elegant appetizer.
Alternative presentations include filo triangles or ramekins.
Makes 12 appetizers.

1 kg (2.2 lbs.) mussels
62 ml ($1/4$ cup) dry white wine
1 small onion, chopped
5 sprigs parsley
500 g (1 lb.) scallops

Sauce
45 ml (3 tbsp.) unsalted butter
90 ml (6 tbsp.) cream
45 ml (3 tbsp.) flour
1 egg yolk
30 ml (2 tbsp.) unsalted butter
250 ml (1 cup) cooked spinach, liquid pressed out and chopped
 (you may substitute frozen)
1.2 ml ($1/4$ tsp.) cayenne pepper
2.5 ml ($1/2$ tsp.) nutmeg
Salt and pepper to taste
125 ml ($1/2$ cup) Parmesan cheese

Place mussels, wine, onion, and parsley in pot. Cover and bring to boil. Boil until mussels open.
Strain the liquid. Reserve 375 ml ($1 1/2$ cups). Remove mussels from their shells. Set aside.

Gently poach scallops in some of the reserved liquid for 1 minute. Remove from liquid and set aside.
To make the sauce, melt the butter, add the flour and cook 2 minutes over low heat. Add cream and
mussel juice, stirring constantly until smooth. Simmer 10 minutes over medium low heat. Beat the
egg yolk and butter together, then add to the sauce and cook over low heat 1 minute, stirring
constantly. Add the cayenne, nutmeg, salt and pepper. Divide sauce into 2 equal parts. Add spinach
to one part and mussels and scallops to the other.

Place a spoonful of spinach mixture on a lightly oiled scallop shell, top with a spoonful of
mussel/scallop mixture. Sprinkle with Parmesan cheese. Place under broiler until browned.

"At this time of the year the weather is so hot that if the fish which are put to dry in the sun were not regularly turned over they could not be prevented from scorching."

~ Part of a letter written by Stephen Parmenius, Hungarian poet who drowned on a voyage from Newfoundland, to a friend in England, 1583

Cod with Cuban Black Bean Sauce

This dish uses black beans in a sauce rather than as an accompaniment to rice as is often found in Cuban cuisine. Try it with other white fish, such as Boston blue or Mako shark.
Serves 6.

750 g (1¹/2 lbs.) cod fillets
Flour for dredging
Olive oil
Salt and pepper

Sauce
130 g (4 oz.) black beans
750 ml (3 cups) spicy clamato juice
30 ml (2 tbsp.) soya sauce
2 to 4 dashes Tabasco
2 cloves garlic, minced
Juice of 1 - 2 lemons

Coat the cod lightly with flour. Sprinkle with salt and pepper. Heat olive oil in frying pan until hot. Lightly brown the cod on both sides. Remove to baking sheet and bake in 350°F oven for about 10 minutes until cooked.

To make the sauce, soak beans overnight in clamato juice. Bring to a boil and simmer 3 hours or until mushy, adding a little water, if needed, to prevent sticking. Purée the black beans in food processor. Place in saucepan. Add the soya sauce, Tabasco, garlic, and lemon. Simmer over medium heat for 15 minutes. Serve with rice.

"...but here they (capelin) are not allowed the least respite, they are captured by millions or driven again into the deep, where there is scarcely a chance of escape for either the parent fish or the ova, and prolific as they are, there is a possibility of their becoming extinct."

- *Journal of the House of Assembly of Newfoundland, 1863*

"A large Pott was put on the Fire and two or three dozen Lobsters were put to death in a few minutes."

- Aaron Thomas, Able Seaman, 1794

A sandwich maker transforms these two toasted sandwiches into sealed pockets with hidden secrets.
Serves 4.

Smoked Salmon & Dill Cheese Sandwich

100 g (4 oz.) smoked salmon, sliced thinly
60 ml (4 tbsp.) cream cheese or Roquefort cheese
Fresh dill sprigs
Lemon
Freshly ground pepper
8 slices bread of your choice
Olive oil or butter

Place the smoked salmon on 4 slices of bread. Chop the dill. Mix together the cheese, dill, lemon juice and pepper to taste. Spread on the remaining 4 slices of bread.

Put the sandwich together and butter or oil the outsides if you want a crusty sandwich. Place in preheated sandwich maker and toast until golden.

Smoked Trout Sandwich with Mustard Dill Sauce

Sandwich
100 g (4 oz.) smoked trout, sliced thinly
Sharp cheddar, sliced thinly
8 slices bread
Unsalted butter

Sauce
30 ml (2 tbsp.) Dijon mustard
15 ml (1 tbsp.) sugar
15 ml (1 tbsp.) white wine vinegar
2.5 ml ($^1/2$ tsp.) dry mustard
62 ml ($^1/4$ cup) vegetable oil
30 ml (2 tbsp.) fresh dill, chopped

To make sauce, blend Dijon mustard, sugar, white wine vinegar, and dry mustard in food processor. While the motor is running, add the oil in a very thin stream. It should be as thick as mayonnaise. Stir in dill.

Spread dill sauce on one side of each slice of bread. Put slices of trout and cheese on one slice. Cover with another slice. Then spread butter on the outside of each sandwich. Place in hot sandwich maker and cook until toasted.

Serve with a green salad and the rest of the dill mustard sauce.

Boiled Lobster

Lobsters were once so common that they were scooped up with a hook from the bow of a small boat to be used as bait. Now they are scarce and harder to catch, but boiling them still only requires a large pot and someone willing to toss them in head first.

500 g (1¼ lbs.) lobster per person
Salted water to cover
Seaweed if possible

Bring salted water and seaweed to a rapid boil. Place lobsters in head first. (This kills them instantly.) Continue to boil 12 to 15 minutes longer. Lobsters are cooked if one of the small side legs pulls off with a twist of the tongs.

Serve hot with melted butter or cold with mayonnaise.

Lobstershell Purée

Don't throw the shells and bodies away. Boil them up with wine and vegetables to make a purée for soups and sauces.

Lobster shells and bodies
  (not the old woman - a lump of bitter
  black stuff up near the head which is
  said to be poisonous), coarsely chopped
1 carrot, chopped
1 onion, chopped
2 shallots, chopped
1 clove garlic, crushed
125 ml (½ cup) unsalted butter
315 ml (1¼ cups) dry white
  wine or vermouth
250 ml (1 cup) water
45 ml (3 tbsp.) tomato paste
6 sprigs parsley
3 sprigs fresh thyme
1 bay leaf

Melt the butter in a saucepan, add vegetables and shells and sauté 5 minutes. Cover and cook over a moderate heat for 10 minutes or until soft. Add wine, water, tomato paste, parsley, thyme and bay leaf. Simmer 30 minutes. Force through a sieve. Refrigerate or freeze for making lobster flavoured sauces.

Note: Added to a reduced cream or white sauce with the addition of your favorite herbs and spices creates a delicious sauce.

Salt Cod Chowder

Although shunned by many as a sign of poverty, salt cod has historically been a mainstay of the Newfoundland diet. Now with its scarcity, cod is likely to join the ranks of sturgeon caviar and black truffles, as food for the rich and famous.

Serves 6 - 8.

650 - 700 g (1 1/2 lbs.) salt cod,
  soaked according to directions
Flour
Olive oil
30 ml (2 tbsp.) olive oil
3 garlic cloves, minced
1 green pepper, cut in strips
1 red pepper, cut in strips
3 onions, coarsely chopped
1 1/4 L (5 cups) fish stock
1.2 ml (1/4 tsp.) crushed
  hot pepper flakes
400 ml (19 oz.) tin tomatoes,
  chopped coarsely
125 ml (1/2 cup) white wine
2.5 ml (1/2 tsp.) dried basil
15 ml (1 tbsp.) fresh chopped parsley
2.5 ml (1/2 tsp.) curry powder
2.5 ml (1/2 tsp.) dried thyme
Salt
Freshly ground pepper

If the salt cod has not been skinned and boned, remove the skin and bones. Pat dry and cut into 3 cm² (1 1/2 -inch) pieces. Dip in flour and fry in olive oil, over medium heat, until tender but not browned. Set aside.

Sauté the onions, garlic, red and green peppers in the 30 ml olive oil. Add the spices, tomatoes, and fish stock. Cover and simmer 15 minutes. Add the wine and simmer 5 minutes. Just before serving add the salt cod, being careful not to let it boil. Serve immediately. This chowder does not improve with age.

> "...Calld Chowder which I believe is Peculiar to this Country tho here it is the Cheif food of the Poorer & when well made a Luxury that the rich Even in England at Least in my opinion might be fond of It is a Soup made with a small quantity of salt Pork cut into Small Slices a good deal of fish and Biscuit Boyled for about an hour...."
>
> - Joseph Banks, 1766

Salmon Ravioli

A versatile dish, salmon ravioli can be served as an appetizer or main course.
Makes 8 large ravioli.

Ravioli
Homemade pasta dough
480 g (1 lb.) boned and skinned salmon, cut into 60 g (2 oz.) pieces
Lemon zest
Lemon juice
Salt and pepper

Sauce
375 ml (1$1/2$ cups) cream
125 ml ($1/4$ cup) dry white wine
62 ml ($1/4$ cup) fish stock
1 small red pepper, diced
Pinch cayenne pepper
Salt and pepper
4 to 5 fresh basil leaves, finely chopped
45 ml (3 tbsp.) butter
45 ml (3 tbsp.) Dijon mustard

To make the ravioli, after putting pasta dough through the final run on the pasta maker, leave it in wide flat strips. Place pieces of salmon at even intervals along the lower half of strip. Sprinkle salmon with salt, pepper, lemon zest, and lemon juice. Moisten edges of pasta with a pastry brush dipped in water. Fold the top half of pasta over the salmon. Press with fingers to seal around the salmon. Cut with a pizza cutter or sharp knife. Repeat until all pasta and salmon have been formed into ravioli. (These freeze well.)

To make the sauce, simmer the cream, wine and fish stock until reduced by $1/3$. Add the red pepper, reduce the heat so it does not boil. Add cayenne, salt and pepper.

Mix together the egg yolk, butter, and mustard. Stir into the cream mixture and heat over gentle heat for 1 minute. Remove from heat and stir in the basil. Spoon over the salmon ravioli.

Arctic Char with Scallop Mousseline baked in Puff Pastry

Arctic char has historically been a food source for Labrador's native population. Now it is also considered a gourmet item in this combination of char, scallops, and spinach.
Serves 6.

1.4 kg (3 lbs.) Arctic char fillets
250 ml (1 cup) fresh spinach leaves, stems removed
454 g (1 lb.) puff pastry

Mousseline
230 g (1/2 lb.) scallops
1 egg
7.5 ml (1 1/2 tsp.) salt
5 ml (1 tsp.) white pepper
Pinch cayenne pepper
125 ml (1/2 cup) cream
5 ml (1 tsp.) dried tarragon
Juice and rind from 1/2 lemon

To make the mousseline, purée the scallops in a food processor until smooth. Add the salt, pepper, cayenne, tarragon, lemon juice and rind. While the machine is running, slowly pour in the cream. Process until well blended.

Place the spinach leaves evenly over half the fillets. Spread the mousseline evenly on top of the spinach. Top with the rest of the fillets.

Roll out the puff pastry to 1/4 -inch thick. Wrap the Arctic char in the pastry, sealing the seams with the lightly beaten egg. Slit the tops and brush with egg.

Bake in a hot oven 425°F for 15 - 25 minutes, depending on thickness of the char.

Mussel Bisque

Blue mussels are still inexpensive due to the success of the aquaculture business.
This traditional bisque of white wine, cream, and vegetables is delicious as a first course,
or served with crusty French bread and salad as a luncheon.
Serves 8 - 10.

500 ml (2 cups) water
750 ml (3 cups) dry white wine
1400 g (3 lbs.) mussels
125 ml (1/2 cup) unsalted butter
1 large onion, finely chopped
1 large leek, minced and rinsed well
2 large carrots, peeled and minced
4 cloves garlic, minced
3 tomatoes, peeled and chopped (may use tinned)
30 ml (2 tbsp.) fresh dill or 5 ml (1 tsp.) dried
45 ml (3 tbsp.) fresh basil or 5 ml (1 tsp.) dried
750 ml (3 cups) cream or milk
Salt and pepper

Wash the mussels, removing any that do not close. Place in pot with 250 ml (1 cup) wine and 500 ml (2 cups) water. Cover and bring to a boil, boiling until the mussels open. Remove the mussels from the shells. Strain and reserve the liquid. Add enough wine to make 1250 ml (5 cups).

Melt the butter in a large saucepan. Sauté the onions, leeks, carrots, and garlic over high heat until onions are translucent. Reduce the heat to low, cover and cook for 20 minutes. Add the tomatoes and cook 5 minutes (if using tinned do not cook any longer). Add the reserved liquid and simmer, uncovered, 15 minutes. Stir in the cream, dill, basil, and mussels. Heat gently. Taste for salt and pepper.

"Also we wanted not of fresh salmons, trouts, lobsters
and other fresh fish brought daily unto us."

- Sir Humphrey Gilbert, 1583

"...there was 9 pounds due me after paying all my expence for the summer supply and I turned over thet to my mother to lay it out to her desposal. Not much after a long toilsome summer but a little better than usual as I have had a fair trile on the fishing line now I was 3 summers fishing out from home 2 summers on the french shore and 4 summers on the labradore and 1 summer on the grand bank and was not very successful in all my undertakings so I thought it was time to leave it off and try something else for my money."

–Capt. John W. Froude, 1863 - 1939

Game, Meat & Poultry

Row 1 (L - R): Caribou with Red Wine Sauce, Red Grapes & Mixed Peppercorns (p.39); Seal & Chick Pea Tamale Pie (p.50); Langosta Manola (p.15). Row 2 (L - R): Partridge with Red Wine & Lapponia (p.48); Salt Cod Chowder (p.25); Newfoundland Pea Soup (p.62). Row 3 (L - R): Mussell Bisque (p.30).

"The low price they got for them (fish), the dearness of Pork and the severity of the winters proved how abortive the design was of making a Fortune in Newfoundland...."

- *Aaron Thomas, Able Seaman, 1794*

Rabbit Braised in Beer & Onions

This rabbit dish which is both slightly sweet and sour, is delicious with pasta.
If you have the time and energy, make ravioli for something completely different.
Serves 6.

3 wild rabbits, cut into 6 pieces (2 hind legs, 2 fore legs, saddle cut into 2 pieces)
450 g (1 lb.) bacon, cut into 1/2-inch strips
1 1/2 L (6 cups) onions, sliced thickly
4 large cloves garlic, minced
2 bottles beer
500 ml (2 cups) chicken stock
45 ml (3 tbsp.) dark brown sugar
10 ml (2 tsp.) thyme
6 crushed juniper berries
15 ml (1 tbsp.) flour
62 ml (1/4 cup) cider vinegar

Wash and dry the rabbit. Fry bacon until crisp. Remove with slotted spoon. Brown rabbit in the
bacon fat. Transfer to casserole. Brown the onions slowly in the bacon fat. Add garlic and sauté
1 minute. Transfer them to the casserole with the rabbit.

Add the stock, brown sugar, thyme, beer, salt, juniper berries and lots of black pepper. Bring to boil,
scraping up bits from the bottom. Add to the casserole.

Cover casserole. Place in 350°F oven for 1 - 1 1/2 hours or until the rabbit is tender. Mix vinegar
with the flour. Stir into the casserole and bake 30 minutes longer.

Serve with oven browned potatoes or pasta.

Variations: Make rabbit ravioli. Remove rabbit from the bones. Reserve 250 g (1/2 lb.). Return rest
to casserole. Mince the reserved rabbit. Place in bowl. Add 125 ml (1/2 cup) broth, 250 ml (1 cup)
fine dry bread crumbs, salt and pepper to taste. Mix thoroughly. Make favorite pasta dough using
2 eggs. Put through pasta machine and cut into 2-inch rounds. Place 5 ml (1 tsp.) rabbit mixture on
round. Moisten edges. Fold in half, pressing edges together to form half moons. Boil 5 minutes in
rapidly boiling salted water. Add to casserole and serve.

Moose or Caribou Bourguignon

Caribou is sweeter, less gamey, and generally more tender than moose.
Both however will make a delicious Bourguignon. Use a hearty Burgundy for best results.
Serves 6.

120 g (1/4 lb.) bacon, sliced into 1/4-inch strips
1 1/2 kg (3 lbs.) moose or caribou stewing meat, cut in 1-inch chunks
3 large onions, sliced
5 ml (1 tsp.) salt
2.5 ml (1/2 tsp) coarse pepper
30 ml (2 tbsp.) flour
500 ml (2 cups) dry red wine, a Burgundy
Stock, preferably home made game stock, but beef will do
15 ml (1 tbsp.) tomato paste
4 cloves garlic, minced
15 ml (1 tbsp.) thyme
1 bay leaf
225 g (1/2 lb.) mushrooms, sliced

To make the Bourguignon, sauté the bacon in a large casserole until crisp. Transfer to a bowl with a slotted spoon. Dry the meat and sauté in the bacon fat until browned on all sides. Fry one layer at a time. Add meat to the bacon. Sauté the onions, adding olive oil if needed.

Return the meat and bacon to the pan with the onions. Sprinkle with salt, pepper and flour. Stir and cook until the flour is browned. Add the wine, stock to just cover the meat, garlic, thyme, bay leaf, and tomato paste. Bring to a simmer, cover and place in a 350°F oven for 2 hours or until meat is tender.

Sauté the mushrooms, add to the casserole. Taste for salt and pepper. Bake 15 minutes longer.

> "…And fill up your stomach with all you can take,
> There's puddin' and 'praties' and venison steak…."
>
> - H. Hardy, Skipper Dick's Feast

Damson Plum Mint Sauce

Gnarled Damson plum trees can be found throughout Newfoundland wherever settlements once stood. This tart sauce with a hint of fresh wild mint, makes a tangy compliment to sweet Newfoundland grown lamb.

Makes 3 cups.

Ingredients
900 g (2 lbs.) Damson plums
130 g (^{3}/4 - I cup) sugar
30 ml (2 tbsp.) chopped fresh mint
Rind and juice of one lemon
I - 3 ml (^{1}/4 - ^{1}/2 tsp.) cinnamon
250 ml (I cup) Newman's Port and/or red wine

Combine all the ingredients in a large heavy saucepan. Bring to a boil and continue to boil gently, stirring often, for 20 minutes or until the plums are very soft. Press through a sieve. The sauce should be as thick as heavy cream. If too thick, thin it with more port or wine. If too thin cook it longer. Taste for sugar and mint. It should be sweet and sour. This sauce keeps up to one month in the refrigerator.

"Sweet creatures,
did you truly understand
The pleasant life you'd live
in Newfoundland. ..."

- Robert Hayman,
third Governor of Guy's
colony at Cupids, 1617

"And though the winter lingering,
Still racks the ragged robe of Spring,
Tradition claims that we this way,
Observe the twenty-fourth of May."

- R.A.Parsons
May 24th (Trouter's Day in Newfoundland)

Caribou with Red Wine Sauce, Red Grapes & Mixed Peppercorns

En Route magazine described this dish as a "...miracle" which "...leads you deep into the barrens." Delicious when cooked medium-rare to medium. The caribou can be prepared in individual portions or as a roast.
Serves 8 - 10.

2 - 3 kg (4 - 5 lbs.) roast of caribou
Bacon
300 g ($^3/4$ lb.) onions
3 large heads of garlic, cut in half
1$^1/2$ L (6 cups) dry red wine
15 ml (1 tbsp.) sugar
9 sprigs fresh parsley
3 sprigs fresh thyme or 5 ml (1 tsp.) dried
1 bay leaf
60 ml (4 tbsp.) red wine vinegar
750 ml (3 cups) beef broth or consomme
90 ml (6 tbsp.) butter
Beurre manie
Mixed peppercorns
Red grapes

To make the sauce, place onions, garlic heads, sugar, parsley, thyme, bay leaf, and red wine in a large pot. Boil until it is reduced to $^1/4$ its original volume. Remove from pan and strain, discarding pulp. Add red wine vinegar to pot and reduce until syrupy. Add the beef broth and reduce by half. Add the sugar and wine reduction and boil together for 5 minutes. Swirl in butter and thicken with beurre manie if needed. It should coat the back of a wooden spoon.

To roast caribou, wrap bacon, 1-inch intervals, around the roast. Place in hot oven 450°F for 10 minutes, then reduce heat to 325°F. Roast 1 hour for medium-rare, longer for medium and well-done.

Roast Loin of Pork with Glazed Apples & Partridgeberry Sauce

The pork loin is flavored with Newman's Port, red wine, cream and partridgeberries. When served with glazed apples it makes an attractive dinner party roast.
Serves 8 - 10.

2.5 kg (5 - 6 lbs.) pork loin roast, center cut
62 ml ($^{1}/4$ cup) olive oil
15 ml (3 tsp.) thyme
15 ml (3 tsp.) rosemary
10 ml (2 tsp.) salt
6 garlic cloves, peeled and slivered
3 bay leaves
250 ml (1 cup) red wine
250 ml (1 cup) chicken stock

4 apples
Clarified butter for sautéing

Sauce
250 ml (1 cup) Newman's Port
250 ml (1 cup) chicken stock
125 ml ($^{1}/2$ cup) red wine
250 ml (1 cup) whipping cream
5 ml (1 tsp.) thyme
190 ml ($^{3}/4$ cup) partridgeberry sauce
30 - 60 ml (2 - 4 tbsp.) red wine vinegar
15 ml (1 tbsp.) grated orange rind

To roast pork, make slits and insert the garlic slivers. Combine the marinade ingredients and rub over the surface of the pork. Let sit 1 hour.

Pour the stock and red wine around the pork. Add the bay leaves. Place in preheated 450°F oven for 10 minutes. Reduce the heat to 350°F and roast another 30 - 40 min./kg (15 - 20 min./lb.).

To make sauce, remove the pork from the pan and degrease the pan juices. Pour in the port and stock and boil until reduced by half. Add the cream and thyme and boil 5 minutes. Stir in the partridgeberry sauce, vinegar to taste, and orange peel.

To make the apples, peel and core the apples and slice into 1 cm (1/2-inch) thick rings. Sauté in butter.

Game Pâté

This country-style pâté can be made from rabbit, caribou, moose, partridge, duck,
or a mixture of game. Use your favorite herbs and spices to create your own pâté.
Serve with different breads, relishes, and chutneys for infinite variety.
Makes 2 loaves.

1 kg (2.2 lbs.) game, caribou, moose, rabbit. etc.
680 g (1 1/2 lbs.) ground pork
1 kg (2.2 lbs.) chicken livers
380 g (3/4 lb.) bacon or prosciutto, cut into 1/4-inch strips
4 eggs
4 large onions, finely chopped
4 large cloves garlic, minced
125 ml (1/2 cup) brandy
10 ml (2 tsp.) coarse black pepper
15 ml (3 tsp.) thyme or rosemary
2.5 ml (1/2 tsp.) each of mace, nutmeg, cinnamon
15 ml (3 tsp.) juniper berries, crushed
Sliced bacon or pork fat to line pans
4 bay leaves

To make the pâté, coarsely grind the game and chicken livers in meat grinder or food processor. Place
in large bowl.

Add bacon, eggs, onions, garlic, brandy, pepper, thyme. mace, nutmeg, cinnamon and juniper berries.
Mix thoroughly.

Line two (9-inch x 5-inch x 2.5-inch) loaf pans with bacon or thinly sliced pork fat. Fill with game
mixture. Cover top with bacon or pork fat. Place 2 bay leaves on top of each pan. Cover tightly
with aluminum foil. Place in baking dish. Fill dish with 1-inch boiling water and bake in 325°F oven
for 3 1/2 hours.

When baked, remove from oven and pour off some of the fat from each pan. Weight tops with
bricks or other heavy objects and allow to cool. Remove from pans, wrap in plastic wrap or waxed
paper and refrigerate or freeze. Serve with tart wild berry relish or chutneys.

Raised Rabbit Pie

Rabbit season is from mid-October through mid-March. In Newfoundland
most rabbit is snared and therefore is free of shot. It freezes and bottles well.
This cold pie is delicious served with partridgeberry relish.
Serves 8 - 10.

Hot water pastry, made with 500 g (1 lb.) all purpose flour or your favorite meat pie pastry
750 g (1 1/2 lbs.) wild rabbit meat, boned and diced
500 g (1 lb.) chicken, skinned, boned and diced
100 g (4 oz.) prosciutto, finely chopped
60 ml (4 tbsp.) chopped parsley
5 ml (1 tsp.) dried thyme
12 juniper berries, crushed
2 cloves garlic, minced
1 medium onion, finely minced
Salt and pepper
75 ml (5 tbsp.) dry red wine
25 g (1 oz.) butter
1 egg, beaten, to glaze
300 ml (1 1/4 cup) jellied chicken stock
15 ml (1 tbsp.) gelatin

Lightly grease a 20 cm (8-inch) springform pan. Roll out 2/3 of the pastry and line the bottom
and sides of the pan. Mix the rabbit, chicken, prosciutto, herbs, onion, garlic, and seasoning together.
Spoon into the lined pan. Pour the wine over and dot with the butter. Roll out the remaining pastry.
Brush the edges of the pie with the beaten egg and cover with pastry. Crimp the edges. Decorate the
top with pastry leaves made from the trimmings.

Brush the top of pie with the beaten egg. Cut a cross in center, fold back edges and insert an aluminum
foil funnel. Bake 450°F for 20 minutes, reduce heat to 325°F, cover with foil and bake 2 hours.
Remove the foil and bake a further 20 minutes.

Meanwhile, heat the jellied stock until it just melts. Stir in gelatin and leave to soften for 2 minutes.
Heat gently until the gelatin dissolves, then pour into pie. Let the pie cool in the tin. Chill until
needed. Remove foil funnel and pan.

Caribou Cabbage Rolls

The juniper berries add a little mystery to these sweet and sour cabbage rolls.
They freeze very well and reheat nicely in the microwave.
Serves 8 - 12.

20 - 24 large cabbage leaves

Filling
1 kg (2 lbs.) ground caribou
300 g (8 oz.) lean bacon
500 ml (2 cups) cooked rice
3 large cloves garlic
2 large onions
60 ml (4 tbsp.) minced parsley
10 ml (2 tsp.) salt
2.5 ml ($1/2$ tsp.) black pepper
1.2 ml ($1/4$ tsp.) cayenne
5 ml (1 tsp.) dried thyme

Sauce
60 ml (4 tbsp.) olive oil
3 large cloves garlic
4 medium onions
2 x 796 ml (28 oz.) tinned tomatoes
335 ml (12 oz.) beer
125 ml ($1/2$ cup) brown sugar
30 ml (2 tbsp.) vinegar
45 ml (3 tbsp.) lemon juice
15 ml (3 tsp.) salt
2.5 ml ($1/2$ tsp.) black pepper
2 bay leaves
2.5 ml (1 tsp.) thyme
15 ml (1 tbsp.) crushed juniper berries

Topping
60 ml (4 tbsp.) honey
60 ml (4 tbsp.) sour cream

To make the filling, mince the garlic, onion, parsley, and bacon in a food processor. Add the other ingredients and mix thoroughly. Set aside.

To make the sauce, mince the garlic and onion in a food processor. Then in a large pan sauté in olive oil.

Add other ingredients to pan and cover. Simmer for 1 hour.

Meanwhile, steam the cabbage leaves until just limp. Form the meat mixture into small patties and place each one in the center of a cabbage leaf. Fold the sides toward the center, then roll the stem end toward the opposite end. Place in a large baking dish, seam side down. Continue until all the meat mixture is used. Pack the rolls together. They may be stacked. Pour the sauce over the cabbage rolls, cover the dish and bake for 1 hour in a 350°F oven.

Mix together the sour cream and honey. Spoon over the cabbage rolls and bake uncovered a further 30 minutes.

Partridge with Red Wine & Lapponia

The Newfoundland partridge is actually Allen's Willow Ptarmigan, not a true partridge. Since they are a land bird, their flavour is gamey, not fishy. This recipe combines the rich flavours of the partridge and the partridgeberry.

Serves 6.

6 partridge, plucked, cleaned and cut in half lengthwise
Salt and pepper
225 g (1/2 lb.) bacon
190 ml (3/4 cup) chopped shallots
190 ml (3/4 cup) Lapponia (lingonberry liqueur)
375 ml (1 1/2 cups) dry red wine
250 ml (1 cup) cream
375 ml (1 1/2 cups) chicken stock
7.5 ml (1 1/2 tsp.) savoury
2 bay leaves
250 ml (1 cup) partridgeberries
Beurre manie

Cover the partridge with water and 62 ml (1/4 cup) vinegar. Let it soak for 30 minutes. Drain and pat dry. Sprinkle with salt and pepper. Fry the bacon in a frying pan. Remove the bacon and discard. Brown the partridge in the bacon fat. Remove to a casserole, breast side down.

Sauté shallots until translucent. Add wine, Lapponia, cream, chicken stock, bay leaves, and savoury. Bring to a simmer. Pour over the partridge and add chicken stock to cover. Bake in 300°F oven for 1 - 2 hours or until tender.

Remove partridge from liquid and keep warm while preparing the sauce. Strain the liquid. Put liquid in pot and boil until reduced to 500 ml (2 cups). Thicken with beurre manie until the sauce coats the back of a spoon. Add the partridgeberries and remove from the heat. To serve pour part of the sauce over the partridge. Pass the rest.

> "...here are Partridges also of two Kinds
> brown and white...these are all good to Eat...."
>
> - Joseph Banks, 1766

Boneless Chicken Breasts with Bakeapples & Lakka Sabayon

This is an elegant and quick dish that is prepared at the last minute.
If serving guests, have all the ingredients prepared and close at hand before they arrive.
Serves 6.

6 x 140 g (5 oz.) boneless breasts of chicken
140 ml (9 tbsp.) minced onions
30 ml (2 tbsp.) olive oil
30 ml (2 tbsp.) clarified butter
Salt
Mixed peppercorns
Bakeapples for garnish

Sabayon
125 - 190 ml (1/2 - 3/4 cups) unsalted butter
2.5 ml (1/2 tsp.) medium curry powder
Pinch of salt
125 ml (1/2 cup) Lakka liqueur*
60 - 125 ml (4 - 8 tbsp.) dry white wine
125 ml (1/2 cup) homemade chicken stock, fat removed
6 egg yolks

Melt butter and olive oil in a frying pan over medium heat. Sauté the onions very briefly, then add chicken breasts and sauté gently 3 minutes per side, sprinkling each side with salt and mixed peppercorns. Remove to platter and keep warm while you prepare the sabayon.

To prepare the sabayon, take a large stainless steel bowl or pot and melt the butter. While whisking continually add the egg yolks and cook until thick and pale. Whisk in the chicken stock and heat until thick. Then whisk in the curry powder, salt, and wine and heat until thick. Lastly, whisk in the Lakka liqueur and as before heat until thick. Take care to whisk continually and not to let mixture get too hot, or else the egg yolks will curdle.

To serve, place chicken breast on plate, spoon the sabayon over and garnish with bakeapples.

* Lakka liqueur is made from bakeapples, or cloudberries as they are known in other parts of the world. If unavailable, apricot brandy can be substituted.

Seal & Chick Pea Tamale Pie

Chili, chick peas, cornmeal and seal are combined in this recipe to produce a pie which the uninitiated can enjoy while acquiring a taste for the strong dark flavour of seal. Since the meat is ground, this chili seal pie is a good way to use all parts of the seal, not just the flippers.
Serves 6.

Chili
120 g (4 oz.) bacon, cut in 1-inch pieces
250 g (2 large) onions, chopped coarsely
4 large cloves of garlic, minced
454 g (1 lb.) ground seal
398 ml (14 oz.) tomato sauce
540 ml (19 oz.) tinned tomatoes, chopped
5 ml (1 tsp.) worcestershire sauce
30 - 60 ml (2 - 4 tbsp.) chili powder
Salt and pepper to taste
540 ml (19 oz.) chick peas, drained

Crust
120 g (3/4 cup) cornmeal
15 ml (1 tbsp.) flour
15 ml (1 tbsp.) sugar
2.5 ml (1/2 tsp.) salt
7.5 ml (11/2 tsp.) baking powder
1 egg, beaten
80 ml (1/3 cup) milk
15 ml (1 tbsp.) vegetable oil

To make chili, sauté the bacon until crisp in a frying pan. Add the onions and garlic. Sauté until transparent. Add the ground seal and fry thoroughly. Stir in chili powder. Add all the other ingredients. Cover and simmer 30 minutes. Transfer to a 2 qt. casserole. Preheat oven to 425°F.

To make the crust, mix together all the dry ingredients. In another bowl, mix together the egg, milk and oil. Stir lightly into the dry ingredients. Pour over the hot chili mixture. Bake 20 - 25 minutes until browned. The crust may sink when poured onto the chili but it will rise to the top when baked.

> "It contain's the hind part of a Seal which was catch'd that morning in Conception Bay. It was taken out of the Pott, I eat some of it and can pronounce it, according to my Palate, not bad eating,...."
>
> - Aaron Thomas, Able Seaman, 1794

The Friendly Invasion

"...25,000 Newfoundland girls married U.S. servicemen between 1941 and 1976...and over 10,000 [Newfoundland civilians] were permanently...."

- John N. Cardoulis

Vegetables
& Grains

Recipe for Spruce Beer
as written by Joseph Banks, 1766

Take a copper that Contains 12 Gallons
fill it as full of the Boughs
of Black spruce as it will hold
Pressing them down pretty tight
Fill it up with water Boil it till
the Rind will strip off the Spruce Boughs
which will waste it about
one third take them out & add to
the water one Gallon of Melasses
Let the whole Boil till the Melasses
are disolvd take a half hogshead
& Put in nineteen Gallons of water
& fill it up with the Essence. Work
it with Barm or Beergrounds & in
Less than a week it is fit to Drink. . . .

Row 1 (L - R): Puréed Potato & Parsnip (p.66); Braised Beets with Coriander (p.59); Caramelized Parsnip (p.66).
Row 2 (L - R): Braised Red Cabbage (p.55); Savoury Carrots & Turnips (p.65).
Row 3 (L - R): Creamed Onions in Vol-au-vent (p.65).

"...it possesses a little shop for the sale of
confectionery and tape...Nets, sails, oiltuns and
anchorchains lie on all hands. Long legged pigs,
goats and scraggy cows dispute supremacy with bare
legged, bareheaded children who play at 'rigbajing'
and other games in the middle of the street."

- David Kennedy, Jr., 1872

Braised Red Cabbage

This dish is easy to prepare, keeps well, looks great and is delicious with pork and game.
Serves 6.

1 kg (2 lb.) red cabbage, sliced thinly
1 medium onion, chopped finely
50 g (1/3 cup) unsalted butter
125 ml (1/2 cup) water
2 apples, peeled, cored and chopped
30 ml (2 tbsp.) Calvados
30 ml (2 tbsp.) partridgeberry jam
Sour cream for garnish (optional)

Melt the butter in a large saucepan. Add the onion and sauté gently until transparent. Add the cabbage and water. Cover and simmer gently for 45 - 60 minutes, until the cabbage is tender. Add the apples and Calvados, cover and cook 10 minutes more. Stir in the partridgeberry jam. Serve.

Fall Vegetables with Aioli

In the late summer and fall, Newfoundland's roadsides and market places abound with locally grown vegetables. Market gardening is a growing business with the variety and quality far surpassing the produce available in the supermarkets during the rest of the year.
Makes 372 ml (1 1/2 cups).

A variety of fresh vegetables, such as small blue potatoes, small beets, onions, green and yellow beans, snow peas, cauliflower, broccoli, carrots, summer squash. Cook the potatoes, beets, and onions until just tender in lightly salted water. Blanch the other vegetables. This heightens their color and makes them crisp.

Aioli

5 cloves garlic, peeled
2 egg yolks
Juice of 1/2 lemon
1.2 ml (1/4 tsp.) salt
Pinch of white pepper
250 ml (1 cup) olive oil
45 - 60 ml (3 - 4 tbsp.) cream

In blender or food processor, purée the egg yolks, lemon juice, salt, pepper, and garlic. While the motor is running, very slowly add the olive oil. As the aioli thickens, the oil may be added more quickly. Add cream, if necessary, to thin to the consistency of thin mayonnaise.

Home Brew Bread

While some people still grow their own hops, most home brewers use kits. Either can be used in home brew bread which is quick and easy. The beer gives it the texture and taste of raised bread.
Makes one loaf.

400 g (3 cups) all purpose flour
15 ml (3 tsp.) baking powder
7.5 ml ($^3/4$ tsp.) salt
1 bottle home brew or regular beer
Cornmeal

To make the bread, mix together flour, baking powder, and salt. Add the beer until a stiff dough is formed. Place in a shallow baking dish sprinkled with cornmeal. Bake 5 minutes in a 425°F oven, then reduce heat to 350°F and bake a further 25 minutes.

Note: This bread can also be cooked on top of the stove in a dutch oven sprinkled with cornmeal. Whole wheat flour can be substituted for all or part of the all purpose flour.

> "...Cabbage & Lettuce Throve surprizingly as did our Radishes & small Sallet carrots & Turnips which especialy the Last were remarkably Sweet...."
>
> – Joseph Banks, 1766

"*The shops are excellent and up-to-date, and the people extremely kind to strangers, especially when they come from the Old Country.*"

- J.G. Millais, naturalist, big game hunter and animal painter, 1903

Braised Beets with Coriander

Beets are another vegetable which keeps well in the root cellar. While they are usually pickled, or boiled and turned into Harvard beets, this recipe shreds them and adds a hint of coriander.
Serves 4.

500 g (1 lb.) beets, peeled and grated
45 ml (3 tbsp.) unsalted butter
1 small onion, finely chopped
30 ml (2 tbsp.) cider vinegar
5 ml (1 tsp.) sugar
5 ml (1 tsp.) ground coriander
Salt to taste

Melt butter in frying pan over moderate heat. Add beets, onion, cider vinegar, sugar, and coriander. Cover and cook over moderate heat 5 to 10 minutes until tender. Taste for salt.

Potato Carrot Rolls

These rolls are delicious when served warm from the oven with a roast turkey or goose.
If savoury or another herb is added, they can be substituted for the stuffing.
Makes 30 buns or 2 loaves.

30 ml (2 tbsp.) yeast
80 ml (1/3 cup) sugar
375 ml (1 1/2 cups) lukewarm
  potato water or milk
115 g (1/2 cup) unsalted butter,
  very soft
15 ml (1 tbsp.) salt
2 eggs
250 ml (1 cup) mashed potatoes,
  room temperature
900 g (7 cups) all purpose flour
750 ml (3 cups) firmly packed
  grated carrots
10 ml (2 tsp.) savoury (optional)

Proof the yeast in the lukewarm potato water or milk. Add the sugar, salt, butter, eggs, mashed potatoes, savoury and 750 ml (3 cups) of the flour. Beat together until smooth. Cover with a clean cloth and let rise in a warm place until doubled. Add the carrots and the rest of the flour to form a soft pliable dough. Knead until smooth and elastic. Place in a greased bowl, turn so the top is greased and cover with the clean cloth. Let rise until doubled. Punch the dough down and form into buns or loaves. Cover and let rise until almost doubled. Bake in a hot oven at 400°F for 20 minutes for the buns or 45 minutes for the loaves.

Refrigerator Jams & Cream Scones

All refrigerator jams are made with a lot less sugar than standard jams. They taste fresher and fruitier but do not have the same keeping qualities. They will keep well in the refrigerator for a week or two. These recipes are very basic; experiment with the amount of sugar, combinations of fruits and berries, and additional ingredients such as lemon or orange rind, liqueurs, and spices until you develop your favourites.

Partridgeberry
250 ml (1 cup) partridgeberries,
  fresh or frozen
62 ml (1/4 cup) sugar
Orange rind (optional)
Lipponia liqueur (optional)

Blueberry
250 ml (1 cup) blueberries,
  fresh or frozen
45 ml (3 tbsp.) sugar
Dash of nutmeg (optional)
Lemon rind (optional)

Gooseberry
250 ml (1 cup) gooseberries, fresh or frozen
62 ml (1/4 cup) sugar

Black Currant
250 ml (1 cup) black currants, fresh or frozen
100 - 125 ml (6 - 8 tbsp.) sugar

Bakeapple
250 ml (1 cup) bakeapples, fresh,
  frozen or bottled
80 ml (1/3 cup) sugar
Lakka liqueur (optional)

Place fruit and sugar in heavy bottomed saucepan. Bring to a boil and boil until it is as thick as you would like it (5 - 10 minutes). Add additional ingredients. Remove from heat. Cool and store in refrigerator.

Cream Scones (12 2-inch scones)
500 ml (2 cups) all purpose flour
15 ml (1 tbsp.) baking powder
30 ml (2 tbsp.) sugar
2.5 ml (1/2 tsp.) salt
62 ml (1/4 cup) butter
2 eggs, lightly beaten, reserve a little
  to brush the tops
80 - 100 ml (1/3 - 1/2 cup) evaporated
  milk or cream
Sugar to sprinkle on tops

Mix together the flour, baking powder, sugar, and salt. Cut in the butter until the mixture resembles fine crumbs. Combine the eggs and milk. Stir into the mixture, adding additional milk if needed, until dough is soft and pliable.

Turn out onto a lightly floured board and knead quickly and gently until dough sticks together. Roll out to 1/2-inch thickness and cut into 2-inch rounds. Place on ungreased baking sheet and brush with the reserved egg. Sprinkle with sugar and bake 10 - 15 minutes in a hot oven 400°F until golden brown.

Newfoundland Pea Soup with Swedish Pancakes & Partridgeberry Sauce

This book would not be complete without Newfoundland pea soup. It is made with salt beef, yellow split peas, turnip and carrot and rivals pea soups from around the world.

600 g (1 1/4 lbs.) salt beef, soaked overnight
450 g (2 1/2 cups) yellow split peas
3 L (12 cups) water
4 medium onions, chopped
500 g (1 lb.) carrots, peeled and
  cut into 1/2-inch pieces
500 g (1 lb.) turnip, peeled and
  cut into 1/2-inch cubes
2 bay leaves
Coarse black pepper

Cut salt beef into small chunks. Place salt beef, peas, water, onions, and bay leaves in a large pot. Cover and bring to a boil. Reduce heat and boil gently for 2 - 3 hours or until thick and creamy. Add turnips, carrots, and pepper. Boil together another 30 minutes, until vegetables are tender.

"The Motto which is riveted on the minds of all Housekeepers here is that He who will not work shall not eat...."

~ Aaron Thomas, Able Seaman, 1794

Swedish Pancakes

Swedish pancakes are slightly thicker than French crêpes but thinner and eggier than North American pancakes. Every Thursday night pea soup, Swedish pancakes and partridgeberry sauce are served for dinner. Serves 8.

4 eggs
500 ml (2 cups) milk or half
  milk and cream
180 g (1 1/3 cups) flour
115 g (1/2 cup) butter, melted
5 ml (1/2 tsp.) salt

Beat eggs and 190 ml (3/4 cup) milk together until well combined. Add the flour and beat until smooth. Beat in the remaining milk, melted butter, and salt. The batter should be the consistency of whipping cream.

Heat a skillet until water sprinkled on it sizzles and evaporates immediately. Drop spoonfuls of batter on the skillet. They should form small 3-inch pancakes and bubble immediately. Cook 1 minute, flip and brown the other side. Serve immediately with warm tart partridgeberry sauce. Makes 48 small 3-inch pancakes.

Partridgeberry Sauce

500 ml (2 cups) partridgeberries, fresh or frozen
125 ml (1/2 cup) sugar
30 ml (2 tbsp.) water

Boil partridgeberries and sugar together until the sugar is dissolved. This should be the consistency of thin jam. Makes 375 ml (1 1/2 cups).

"But with the setting up of schools,
and through the influence of
missionaries, teachers, and magistrates,
the Newfoundland character became
temperate, religious, and law-abiding."

– "In the Very Early Days of Settlement"

Savoury Carrots & Turnips

At one time every family had a root cellar full of their home grown potatoes and vegetables in the winter and iceberg ice in the summer. Carrots and turnips would have been among the winter keepers with savoury dried in the late fall. This recipe combines their flavours.
Serves 6.

360 g (1 lb.) turnip, weighed after peeling
340 g (1 lb.) carrots, weighed after peeling
2.5 ml (1/2 tsp.) salt
150 ml (1/2 cup) water
45 ml (3 tbsp.) unsalted butter
3 - 7 ml (3/4 - 11/2 tsp.) savoury
Salt and pepper

Place turnips, carrots, salt and water in a saucepan. Cover and bring to a boil. Reduce heat and simmer gently 15 - 20 minutes until tender.

Remove from heat. Do not drain. Mash. Add butter, savoury, salt and pepper to taste. Makes 3 cups.

Creamed Onions in Vol-au-Vent

As an alternative to the vol-au-vent shells, you can bake large choux shells and fill them with the creamed onions. This makes a light lunch when topped with blue or Parmesan cheese and served with a green salad.
Serves 6.

Onions
500 g (6 medium) onions, peeled and
  cut into 1/4-inch pieces
2.5 ml (1/2 tsp.) salt
250 ml (1 cup) water
6 baked vol-au-vent shells

Sauce
30 ml (2 tbsp.) unsalted butter
30 ml (2 tbsp.) flour
250 ml (1 cup) liquid
  (onion liquid plus milk or cream)
2.5 ml (1/2 tsp.) nutmeg
2.5 ml (1/2 tsp.) salt
1.25 ml (1/4 tsp.) cayenne pepper

Cook the onions, water and salt together in a covered saucepan until tender, approximately 15 minutes. Drain, reserving liquid.

To make sauce, melt the butter in a saucepan. Add the flour and stir one minute over medium low heat. Slowly whisk in the liquid. Bring to the boil, then reduce heat immediately to low. Stir in seasonings. Mix in onions.

Fill vol-au-vent shells and place under broiler to brown.

Variations: Top with your favorite cheese before placing under broiler.

Puréed Potato & Parsnip

The best parsnip is left in the ground until spring when it becomes delightfully sweet.
This purée slips down very easily, so make lots.
Serves 6 - 8.

300 g (10 oz.) peeled parsnip,
  cut into large chunks
500 g (1 1/4 lbs.) peeled potatoes,
  cut into chunks
2.5 ml (1/2 tsp.) salt
250 ml (1 cup) water
2 large garlic cloves, peeled and mashed
30 ml (2 tbsp.) olive oil
2.5 ml (1/2 tsp.) cumin
2.5 ml (1/2 tsp.) curry powder
Milk or cream, if needed

Place the potatoes, parsnip, garlic, salt, and water in a saucepan. Cover and bring to a boil. Reduce heat and simmer until very tender, approximately 20 minutes.

Do not drain. (There should be very little liquid remaining in the saucepan.) Mash. Add the olive oil, cumin, and curry powder. Mash until smooth. Add milk or cream if it seems too thick. Taste for salt and pepper.

Variations: With the addition of more milk and cream this becomes a vichyssoise. Garnish with chopped parsley and chives.

Caramelized Parsnip

Parsnip is an unappreciated vegetable. Caramelized parsnips are easy to prepare
and delicious, two qualities which should bring them more prominence.
Serves 4.

1 kg (2.2 lbs.) parsnip, peeled and cut into
  1 cm (1/2-inch) thick pieces,
  5 - 8 cm (2- to 3-inches) long
2.5 ml (1/2 tsp.) salt
45 ml (3 tbsp.) unsalted butter
60 ml (4 tbsp.) brown sugar

Cook parsnip in water and salt until just tender, 10 minutes. Drain and place in lightly buttered shallow baking dish.

Meanwhile, melt the butter. Add the brown sugar and stir until the sugar is dissolved and the mixture looks smooth and creamy. Pour butter/sugar mixture over the cooked parsnip. Place in a hot oven, 400°F for 10 minutes or until bubbling and slightly caramelized.

"...but most stayed and within months the blackened,
fire scarred town had once again raised itself from the
ashes, a fabulous Phoenix that just refused to die."

- Captain David Buchan speaking
about the St. John's Fire of 1892.

Desserts

> *"It would do us good," he said.*
> *"When strangers came, he commonly*
> *had a bit of tea."*
>
> *- Rev. Louis L. Noble, 1859*

Row 1 (L - R): Ginger Bakeapple Tart (p.79); Three Berry Newfoundland Torte (p.84); Framboise Chocolate Mousse Cake (p.76). Row 2 (L - R): Marsh Berry Rhubarb Pie (p.90); Chilled Blueberry Pecan Cheesecake (p.75); Mid-Winter Pie (p.81). Row 3 (L - R): Tulips with Pastry Cream & Fresh Berries (p.71).

"*For centuries, the talents and creativity of Newfoundlanders have been dammed up by hardship and poverty. That is ended. From now on, Newfoundlanders will make a contribution to Canada out of all proportion to their numbers.*"

- Rt. Hon. J.W.Pickersgill, P.C., C.C.
at his farewell dinner in St. John's, 1967

Tulips with Pastry Cream & Fresh Berries

These must be assembled at the last minute or the delicate crisp tulips will turn soggy.
They take only a moment to put together and are almost too beautiful to eat.
Serves 8 - 10.

Tulips
80 g (6 tbsp.) unsalted butter,
  room temperature
60 g (1/4 cup) sugar
60 g (1/2 cup) flour, sifted
2.5 ml (1/2 tsp.) vanilla extract
2 egg whites

Pastry Cream
250 ml (1 cup) milk
1/4 vanilla bean or 2.5 ml
  (1/2 tsp.) vanilla
80 ml (1/3 cup) sugar
3 egg yolks
30 ml (2 tbsp.) cornstarch
250 ml (1 cup) heavy cream, whipped
45 ml (3 tbsp.) Grand Marnier

Fruit
250 - 375 ml (1 - 1 1/2 cups)
  fresh berries
Sugar to taste
Juice of lemon, lime, or orange to taste
15 ml (1 tbsp.) liqueur,
  appropriate to particular berry

To make tulips, beat sugar and butter together until light and creamy. Beat in flour and vanilla. Beat egg whites until they stand in stiff peaks. Fold into creamed mixture.

Brush surface of baking sheet with butter. Mark out 5-inch diameter circles, 2 or 3 per pan. Spoon 15 ml (1 tbsp.) batter into center of circle and smooth evenly into a thin layer to cover the circle.

Bake in a preheated 425°F oven for 3 minutes, watching closely to prevent burning. Remove from oven and immediately remove from sheet and push gently into a cup. Let cool completely in the cup. Continue until all batter is used. Store in a cool dry place.

To make pastry cream, bring milk and vanilla bean to boil. Cover and keep warm.

Beat sugar and egg yolks until mixture forms a ribbon. Stir in cornstarch. While beating egg/sugar mixture pour in the hot milk. Pour mixture back into saucepan and bring to a boil, stirring constantly. Cook for 1 minute. Remove from heat and add vanilla extract, if used. Cover and let cool. Fold in whipped cream and Grand Marnier.

To prepare fruit, gently stir together the berries, sugar, citrus juice and liqueur. Let sit 1 hour or until ready to serve.

To serve, place tulip on plate, spoon in pastry cream, top with marinated berries. Serve at once.

Note: Bakeapples are very good marinated in Lakka, blueberries in an orange flavoured liqueur, gooseberries in cassis.

Partridgeberry Sorbet

Partridgeberries grow wild over the hills of Newfoundland and Labrador. They are so acidic that they can be kept all winter long in jars or barrels covered with water. Raw, they are nearly inedible, but cooked, they are unsurpassed in taste and variety of uses from game dishes to desserts.
Makes 1 L (1 qt.).

400 g (2 cups + 2 tbsp.) sugar
160 ml (2/3 cup) water
500 g (4 cups) partridgeberries, fresh or frozen
2 tart apples, peeled, cored, and puréed
Rind of 2 oranges
30 ml (2 tbsp.) Calvados
1 egg white

Heat the water, sugar, and berries together until the berries are tender. Purée and press through a sieve. Add the puréed apples, orange rind, and Calvados. Put in freezer until firm.

Beat the egg white until soft peaks form. Purée the frozen fruit mixture in a food processor. Fold in the egg white and freeze until firm.

Bakeapple Sorbet

This pale apricot colored sorbet contains the rich musty flavor of the bakeapple without its many seeds. Lakka liqueur enhances this light lovely sorbet.
Makes 1.5 L (1.75 qts.).

1 L (2 pts.) bakeapples
750 ml (3 cups) water
280 g (1 3/4 cups) sugar
Zest of 1 orange
Zest and juice of 1/2 lemon
100 ml (7 tbsp.) orange juice
30 ml (2 tbsp.) Lakka liqueur*
60 ml (4 tbsp.) cream
1 egg white

Place bakeapples, water, and sugar in saucepan. Place over high heat and bring to a boil. Turn heat down and simmer until berries are tender, approximately 10 minutes.

Cool, then purée and press through sieve. Add zest and juice of orange and lemon, Lakka liqueur, and cream. Freeze until firm. Beat the egg white until soft peaks form.

Place the bakeapple sorbet in food processor with the beaten egg white and process until smooth. Freeze.

* Lakka liqueur is made from bakeapples, or cloudberries as they are known in other parts of the world. If unavailable, apricot brandy can be substituted.

Blueberry Sorbet

Wild blueberries are Newfoundland's main exported fruit. They have more flavour than any other blueberry in the world. Serve alone, or in combination with partridgeberry and bakeapple sorbets, and enjoy Newfoundland's three most popular berries together.

Makes 1 L (1 qt.).

1 L (2 pts.) blueberries
280 g (1³/4 cups) sugar
500 ml (2 cups) water
Zest and juice of 1 lime
120 ml (¹/2 cup) orange juice
180 ml (²/3 cup) light red wine,
  such as Beaujolais
1.2 - 2.5 ml (¹/4 - ¹/2 tsp.) nutmeg
1 egg white

Place blueberries, sugar, and water in saucepan. Bring to boil and simmer gently until berries are tender. Remove from heat and let cool slightly. Press through sieve. Add zest and juice of lime, orange juice, red wine, and nutmeg. Cool completely, then freeze until firm. Beat egg white until soft peaks form. Place blueberry mixture in food processor and process till mushy. Fold in beaten egg white. Freeze.

"…in the Lower Garden was the Cemetery…, for in the Grave perhaps lay the Ashes of one who once gave Pleasure to the eye, Satisfaction to the Heart, Gratitude to the Senses, Information to the Ignorant, Cheerfulness to the mind and Mirth to the circle."

- Aaron Thomas, Able Seaman, 1794

"I have heard my neighbours mutter
About a substitute called butter...
He says Joe would expose the nation
To this strange, bovine creation,
And pass a law ~ now can you beat it ~
Compelling everyone to eat it!"

- Gregory J. Power
"The Ballad of Oleo Margarine"

Chilled Blueberry Pecan Cheesecake

This untraditional, uncooked cheesecake combines tangy lemon curd, delicate blueberries, and crunchy pecans. It is a taste and texture treat to end a lobster or scallop dinner.
Serves 12.

Lemon Curd

6 egg yolks
250 ml (1 cup) sugar
125 ml (1/2 cup) lemon juice
125 ml (1/2 cup) butter, in pieces
15 ml (1 tbsp.) lemon rind

Beat together egg yolks, lemon juice, and sugar. Place over simmering water and beat until thick and creamy and coats back of wooden spoon. Remove from heat and stir until slightly cooled. Beat in butter, one piece at a time. Stir in lemon rind. Cool completely.

Fatfree Sponge or Genoise

4 whole eggs
100 g (3/4 cup) sugar
100 g (scant 1 cup) flour, sifted

Beat eggs and sugar slightly. Place over simmering water and beat until thick and creamy and ribbon falls back on itself (10 minutes). Remove from heat and beat until ribbon remains on batter for at least 5 seconds (5 - 10 minutes). Fold in flour in thirds. Pour into greased and floured springform pan and bake at 350°F for 30 minutes in an 81/2-inch pan, 20 minutes in an 91/2-inch pan.

Cheesecake

30 ml (2 tbsp.) Grand Marnier mixed
  with 45 ml (3 tbsp.) orange juice
375 g cottage cheese
250 ml (1 cup) lemon curd
80 ml (1/3 cup) sugar
30 ml (2 tbsp.) Grand Marnier
30 ml (2 tbsp.) orange zest
125 ml (1/2 cup) chopped pecans
500 ml (2 cups) blueberries
440 ml (13/4 cups) cream,
  softly whipped
2 envelopes gelatin, dissolved in
  80 ml (1/3 cup) cold water

Grease 91/2-inch springform pan. Slice genoise in half crosswise. Place one half on bottom of pan and brush with Grand Marnier and water mixture. (Use the other half for something else or freeze.) Dissolve gelatin over hot water. Purée cottage cheese and mix together with lemon curd, sugar, Grand Marnier, orange zest, pecans and dissolved gelatin. Fold in whipped cream. When slightly firm, fold in blueberries and pour into genoise lined pan. Refrigerate. Garnish with chopped pecans.

Variation: Substitute 375 ml (11/2 cups) partridge-berries for blueberries and 75 ml (5 tbsp.) pistachios for pecans.

Framboise Chocolate Mousse Cake

This chocolate mousse and raspberry liqueur cake is too tempting to resist.
Fill the center with fresh raspberries and serve with whipped cream for a really festive dessert.
Serves 16 - 20.

Pound Cake
250 g (1 cup) butter
250 g (1²/3 cups) sugar
4 large eggs
125 g (1 cup) flour
125 g (1¹/3 cups) potato flour
5 ml (1 tsp.) baking powder
30 ml (2 tbsp.) Framboise
5 ml (1 tsp.) lemon zest
375 ml (1¹/2 cups) orange juice
45 - 60 ml (3 - 4 tbsp.) Framboise
15 ml (1 tbsp.) sugar

Cream together butter and 1/2 the sugar until light and fluffy. Add Framboise and lemon zest. Beat in, one at a time, 1 whole egg and 3 egg yolks. Sift together the flours and baking powder. Stir into the butter mixture, 45 ml (3 tbsp.) of the flour mixture at a time. Do not beat. Beat egg whites until firm, beat in rest of sugar and continue beating until satiny and smooth. Lighten batter by stirring in 3 spoonfuls of the egg whites, then fold in the rest. Pour into greased and floured bundt pan. Bake at 350°F for 45 - 60 minutes. Let cool in pan 10 minutes. Turn out and cool completely.

To assemble divide into three layers. Place 1/3 in bottom of bundt pan and brush with 1/3 orange juice and Framboise mixture. Spoon in 1/2 of the chocolate mousse (recipe follows). Place next cake layer on top of mousse and brush with 1/3 orange juice mixture. Spoon in the rest of chocolate mousse and finish with last cake layer and orange juice mixture. Refrigerate overnight. Cover with chocolate icing (recipe follows).

Chocolate Mousse

4 eggs, separated
190 ml (3/4 cup) sugar
62 ml (1/4 cup) combination
  Framboise and orange liqueur
6 oz. semisweet chocolate
60 ml (4 tbsp.) cream
6 oz. unsalted butter
Pinch of salt
15 ml (1 tbsp.) sugar

Beat sugar and yolks together until thick and pale. Place over simmering water. Beat in liqueur. Beat until thick and too hot to touch. Beat over cold water until a ribbon forms.

Melt chocolate and cream over hot water. Remove from heat and beat in butter, one piece at a time. Then beat into first mixture.

Beat whites and salt till soft peaks form. Sprinkle on sugar and beat until stiff. Stir 1/4 into chocolate mixture, then fold in the rest.

Icing

6 oz. semisweet chocolate
90 ml (6 tbsp.) butter
15 ml (1 tbsp.) Framboise

Melt over simmering water. Remove from heat and beat until pourable/spreadable.

"Of late years, however, taste has been developing and houses have been built of a superior description. Gradually the wooden buildings will be replaced by houses built on the best of models...."

- Rev. Moses Harvey, St. John's, 1883

"Hurrah for our own native Isle, Newfoundland,
Not a stranger shall hold one inch of its strand,
Her face turns to Britain, her back to the Gulf,
Come near at your peril Canadian Wolf."

- Anti-Confederation Song, 1946 - 1949

Ginger Bakeapple Tart

Crystallized ginger and ginger snaps are the surprise ingredients in this tart.
Serve as a dessert after a dinner party or enjoy with morning coffee.
Serves 8.

Crust
500 ml (2 cups) finely ground ginger snaps
110 g (1/2 cup) butter, melted

Filling
250 g (8 oz.) cream cheese
45 ml (3 tbsp.) sugar
45 ml (3 tbsp.) milk
15 ml (1 tbsp.) crystallized ginger,
  finely chopped
Pinch of salt

Topping
500 ml (1 pt.) fresh or frozen bakeapples
62 g (1/3 cup) sugar
30 ml (2 tbsp.) Lakka liqueur

To make the crust, combine the ground ginger snaps and butter. Press into a 9-inch springform pan. Bake 8 - 10 minutes in a 350°F oven. Cool completely.

To make the filling, beat all the ingredients together until light and fluffy. Pour into cooled crust and refrigerate until firm.

To make the topping, combine bakeapples and sugar in a saucepan. Bring to a boil and boil gently until thickened, approximately 5 - 10 minutes. Add liqueur and remove from heat. Cool completely.

Spread the topping evenly over the cream cheese filling. Refrigerate.

"My life when I glance back over my pass
Time and call to mind the ups and downs the
Calms and storms the pleasures and enjoyments
And all the changing sceens that nature can
Produce and now here in just about the
Same circumstances as when a boy of eight
Years therfore I belive that life is a lotery."

- Capt. John W. Froude, 1863 - 1939

Mid-Winter Pie

Turnip and carrots make pumpkin pie and sweet potato pie lovers rethink their meaning.
Use equal quantities of leftover cooked turnips and carrots for the best result.
Makes one 9-inch pie.

480 ml (2 cups) puréed turnip and carrots
45 ml (3 tbsp.) unsalted butter, melted and cooled
1.25 ml ($1/4$ tsp.) nutmeg
2.5 ml ($1/2$ tsp.) cinnamon
2.5 ml ($1/2$ tsp.) allspice
2 eggs, slightly beaten
250 ml (1 cup) evaporated milk
80 ml ($1/3$ cup) packed brown sugar
Grated rind of 1 orange
Pastry for 1 9-inch pie plate

Line the bottom of pie plate with the pastry. Crimp the edges. Poke holes in the bottom with the tines of a fork.

Mix all the other ingredients together. Pour into the unbaked pie shell. Place in oven and bake 10 minutes at 450°F, then reduce heat to 350°F for a further 30 minutes or until a knife inserted into center comes out clean. Cool on wire rack.

"...I was born in a
Mean cottage on the side of a weather
Beatin hill where the winds roar...."

- Capt. John W. Froude, 1863 - 1939

Newfoundland Spotted Dick
with Newman's Port Sabayon

The English Navy survived on Spotted Dick made with raisins.
This version surpasses "survival." The rich buttery Port sabayon
transports the tart partridgeberry steamed pudding to heights fit for HRM.
Serves 8 - 10.

Dick
115 g ($^{1}/2$ cup) butter
160 ml ($^{2}/3$ cup) sugar
2 eggs
260 g (2$^{1}/4$ cups) flour
12 ml (2$^{1}/2$ tsp.) baking powder
1.2 ml ($^{1}/4$ tsp.) salt
2.5 ml ($^{1}/2$ tsp.) nutmeg
Rind and juice of one orange
80 ml ($^{1}/3$ cup) milk
140 g (1$^{1}/2$ cups) partridgeberries, fresh or frozen

Port Sabayon
227 g (1 cup) butter
120 ml ($^{1}/2$ cup) sugar
1.2 ml ($^{1}/4$ tsp.) salt
8 egg yolks
60 ml ($^{1}/4$ cup) water
240 ml (1 cup) Newman's Port

Combine the flour, baking powder, salt, nutmeg, and rind. Remove one tablespoon and mix this with the partridgeberries.

Cream together the butter and sugar until light and fluffy. Add the eggs, one at a time, beating well after each addition. Add the dry ingredients alternately with the orange juice and milk. Stir in the rind, then fold in the partridgeberries.

Spoon mixture into greased 1 L (1 qt.) mold or 8 individual molds. Cover with lid or aluminum foil. Place on rack in deep pot. Add boiling water up to half the height of the molds. Cover the pot with a lid. Boil large mold 1$^{1}/2$ hours or small molds 35 minutes. Remove from pot and allow to cool slightly on wire rack before turning out.

Serve warm with sauce. If cooled completely, may be frozen and reheated in the microwave.

For the sabayon, melt the butter in a large pot or heavy stainless steel bowl. Add the sugar and heat gently until it dissolves. Whisk in the egg yolks and whisk continually until thick and pale. Whisk in the water and salt. When it is thick, whisk in the Newman's Port until thick as cream. Serve immediately or reheat very gently over simmering water.

Three Berry Newfoundland Torte

This is an adaptation of the Icelandic Vinaterta which has a prune filling.
Serve in thin slices with whipped cream. May be frozen and thawed repeatedly. Serves 30 - 40.

Cakes
225 g (I cup) unsalted butter
240 g (I1/2 cups) sugar
3 eggs
45 ml (3 tbsp.) light cream
5 ml (I tsp.) almond extract
500 g (scant 4 cups) all purpose flour, sifted
5 ml (I tsp.) baking powder
Pinch of salt
2.5 ml (1/2 tsp.) nutmeg
2.5 ml (1/2 tsp.) cinnamon
80 g (I cup) ground almonds

Blueberry Filling
300 g (I cup) thick refrigerator blueberry jam
1.2 ml (1/4 tsp.) nutmeg
Juice and rind of 1/2 orange
Juice and rind of 1/2 lime

Bakeapple Filling
380 g (I cup) thick refrigerator bakeapple jam
1.2 ml (1/4 tsp.) cinnamon
Juice and rind of I orange

Partridgeberry Filling
300 g (I cup) thick refrigerator partridgeberry jam
Juice and rind of I orange

Butter Cream
6 egg yolks
200 g (2 cups) confectioners' sugar
400 g (I3/4 cups) unsalted butter, softened
5 ml (I tsp.) almond extract

Garnish
Toasted sliced almonds
Confectioners' sugar

To make the almond cakes, butter and flour 4 x 270 cm (91/2-inch) spring form pans. Set aside.
Combine the flour, baking powder, salt, nutmeg, cinnamon, and ground almonds in a bowl.

In another bowl, cream the butter until light and fluffy. Gradually beat in sugar. Add the eggs, one at
a time, beating well after each addition. Add 1/2 of the dry ingredients, then the cream. Mix in the
rest of the dry ingredients. Divide the dough into 4 pieces. Pat evenly into prepared pans. Roll lightly
with floured rolling pin to smooth tops. Bake at 350°F for 15 - 20 minutes, being careful not to
over bake.

To make the blueberry filling, combine all ingredients. Repeat for the bakeapple filling and the
partridgeberry filling (they must be as thick as jam).

To make the buttercream icing, place all ingredients in a mixing bowl and beat together until smooth.

To assemble, place a layer of almond cake on cake plate and spread with I cup of blueberry filling.
Top with a layer of almond cake. Spread I cup of bakeapple filling over this and top with another
layer of cake. Then spread I cup of partridgeberry filling over this layer. Place the last layer of cake
on top. Spread the icing over the top and sides of the torte. Smooth the top. Cover the sides with
sliced toasted almonds. Sift confectioners' sugar over the top and score with a long metal spatula.

"These Dogs, in Summer, lead the perfect life of an Idler.
They do no kind of work whatever."

- Aaron Thomas, Able Seaman, 1794

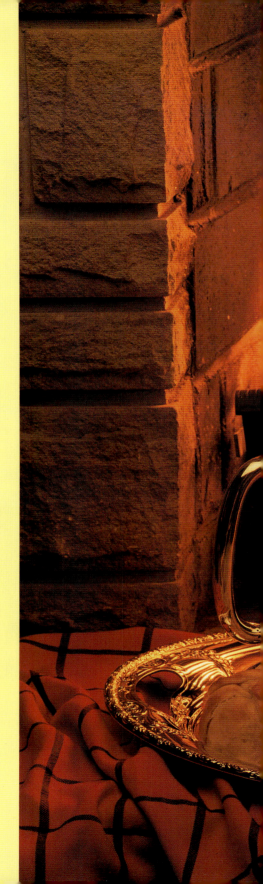

Apple Partridgeberry Bourdelot

Decorate these apples with pastry leaves and a piece of
cinnamon stick so they resemble apples.
Serve them cold, warm, or hot from the oven with
Calvados scented whipped cream or ice cream.
Makes 8 apples.

500 g (4 cups) flour
350 g (1³/4 cups) unsalted butter, room temperature
2 eggs, slightly beaten
45 - 75 ml (3 - 5 tbsp.) milk
25 ml (1¹/2 tbsp.) icing sugar
5 ml (1 tsp.) salt
8 apples
125 ml (¹/2 cup) sugar mixed with
  30 ml (2 tbsp.) cinnamon
125 ml (¹/2 cup) partridgeberry jam
  mixed with 15 ml (1 tbsp.) Calvados

To make pastry, mix together flour, salt and icing sugar.
Cut in the butter until it looks like cornmeal. Add the
beaten eggs and milk and mix together until it is
smooth. Roll out and cut into star shapes large enough
to wrap around the apples.

Peel and core apples, leaving some apple in the bottoms.
Roll in sugar/cinnamon mixture. Fill centers with
Calvados flavoured partridgeberry jam. Place on center
of pastry. Fold pastry up and around apple. Brush with
beaten egg yolk and milk. Bake 375°F for 15 - 20 minutes.

Rhubarb Sauce

Some people eat this first "fruit" to appear in the spring as a vegetable.
No matter how it is served it is a welcomed sign that winter is over. Serve warm or cold over
Ruby's ice cream, churned in an old fashion hand turned ice cream maker and iceberg ice.
Makes 1 L (1 qt.).

1 kg (2 lbs.) rhubarb, cut into 1-inch pieces
180 g (1 cup) sugar
15 - 30 ml (1 - 2 tbsp.) finely chopped crystallized ginger

To make the sauce, place washed rhubarb in a saucepan with a heavy bottom. Cover and bring to a
boil over a medium low heat. Add the sugar and ginger and boil 1 minute more or until sugar is
dissolved. Cool and refrigerate.

Ruby's Ice Cream

Don't let the ingredients influence you. This ice cream is as rich and creamy as
Haagen Daas, at a fraction of the cost. Ruby could "put a good taste on anything."
Makes 2 qts.

3 x 385 ml (14 oz.) tins evaporated milk + 2 tins water
360 g (2 cups) sugar
56 g (2 packages) custard powder
15 ml (1 tbsp.) vanilla
10 ml (2 tsp.) lemon flavouring
5 ml (1 tsp.) salt
368 ml (14 oz.) tinned crushed pineapple

To make custard, place milk, water and sugar in saucepan. Stir in the custard powder and bring to a
boil, stirring continually. Boil 1 minute. Remove from heat and add pineapple with its juice, vanilla,
lemon flavouring, and salt. Cool completely.

To make ice cream, place in ice cream freezer and follow freezer directions.

Marsh Berry Rhubarb Pie

Marsh berries are small cranberries found in the bogs of Newfoundland and Labrador.
If you are not a berry picker, keep an eye out for them in small outport shops,
otherwise substitute partridgeberries or imported cranberries.
One 9-inch pie.

Crust for double crusted 9-inch pie

Filling
450 g (4 cups) fresh or frozen rhubarb, cut into pieces
250 g (2 cups) fresh or frozen marsh berries or cranberries
225 g (1 1/4 cups) sugar
62 ml (1/4 cup) flour
Grated rind of 1 orange
15 ml (1 tbsp.) unsalted butter
15 ml (1 tbsp.) crystallized ginger, finely chopped

To make filling, mix rhubarb, marsh berries, sugar, flour, orange rind, and ginger together.

Line the bottom of pie plate with pastry, fill with the fruit mixture, and dot with butter.
Cover with pastry. Crimp the edges and put slits in the top. Bake in preheated 425°F oven for
10 minutes. Reduce heat to 375°F and bake a further 35 - 55 minutes.

> "Life, in fact, is quite safe as long as you keep clear of
> ...'bert pie.' ...it is so horribly good that many
> helpings are sure to follow in rapid succession, to the
> ultimate ruin of one's digestion."
>
> - J.G. Millais, 1904

*"One of their principal means of excitement
is a free use of stimulating drinks."*

*- Ephriam W. Tucker,
a young American missionary student, 1838*

Notes

(Arranged in order according to quote's appearance in book.)

Thomas, Aaron. *The Newfoundland Journal of Aaron Thomas 1794.* Edited by Jean M. Murray. Longman's Canada Limited, 1968, p. 74.

The Newfoundland Weather Centre of Environment Canada.

Thomas, Aaron. *The Newfoundland Journal of Aaron Thomas 1794.* Edited by Jean M. Murray. Longman's Canada Limited, 1968, p. 69.

Durgin, George Francis. "I Never Sold a Fish for Money Before." *The Newfoundland Character: An Anthology of Newfoundland & Labrador Writings.* Edited by D.W.S. Ryan and T.P. Rossiter. St. John's: Jesperson Press, 1984, p. 103.

Blackmore, Kevin and Johnson, Ray. "Makin' for the Harbour." Buddy Wasisname and the Other Fellers: *Songbook 1.* Kevin Blackmore, Wayne Chaulk and Ray Johnson. Vinland Music, 1991.

Pratt, E.J. "The Depression Ends." *Selected Poems by E.J. Pratt.* Edited by Peter Buitenhuis. Toronto: Macmillan of Canada, 1968, Reprinted 1969, 1972, 1977, p. 22.

Quinn, David B. and Cheshire, Neil M. *The New Found Land of Stephen Parmenius: The life and writings of a Hungarian poet, drowned on a voyage from Newfoundland, 1583.* Toronto: University of Toronto Press, 1972, p. 171.

Newfoundland. Journal of the House of Assembly of Newfoundland. James Seaton, Printer, St. John's. Printed at the office of the "Newfoundland Express," 1863, p. 541.

Thomas, Aaron. *The Newfoundland Journal of Aaron Thomas 1794.* Edited by Jean M. Murray. Longman's Canada Limited, 1968, p. 67.

Lysaght, A.M. *Joseph Banks in Newfoundland & Labrador, 1766: His Diary, Manuscripts and Collections.* Berkeley and Los Angeles: University of California Press, 1971, p. 137.

Gosling, William Gilbert. *The Life of Sir Humphrey Gilbert: England's First Empire Builder.* Westport, Connecticut: Greenwood Press, Publishers, p. 286.

Froude, Capt. John W. *On the High Seas: The Diary of Capt. John W. Froude Twillingate -1863 - 1939.* St. John's: Jesperson Press, 1983, p. 15.

Thomas, Aaron. *The Newfoundland Journal of Aaron Thomas 1794.* Edited by Jean M. Murray. Longman's Canada Limited, 1968, p. 110.

Thomas, Aaron. *The Newfoundland Journal of Aaron Thomas 1794.* Edited by Jean M. Murray. Longman's Canada Limited, 1968, p. 109.

Hardy, H. "Skipper Dick's Feast." *The Newfoundland Character: An Anthology of Newfoundland & Labrador Writings.* Edited by D.W.S. Ryan and T.P. Rossiter. St. John's Jesperson Press, 1984, p. 30.

The Book of Newfoundland volume II. Edited by J.R. Smallwood. Newfoundland Book Publishers, Ltd., 1937, p. 329.

Parsons, R.A. "May 24th (Trouter's Day in Newfoundland)." *The Newfoundland Character: An Anthology of Newfoundland & Labrador Writings.* Edited by D.W.S. Ryan and T.P. Rossiter. St. John's Jesperson Press, 1984, p. 138.

Lysaght, A.M. *Joseph Banks in Newfoundland & Labrador, 1766: His Diary, Manuscripts and Collections.* Berkeley and Los Angeles: University of California Press, 1971.

Thomas, Aaron. *The Newfoundland Journal of Aaron Thomas 1794.* Edited by Jean M. Murray. Longman's Canada Limited, 1968, pp. 65-6.

Cardoulis, John N. *A Friendly Invasion II: A Personal Touch.* St. John's: Creative Publishers, 1993, pp. 3, 11.

Lysaght, A.M. *Joseph Banks in Newfoundland & Labrador, 1766: His Diary, Manuscripts and Collections.* Berkeley and Los Angeles: University of California Press, 1971, pp. 139-40.

O'Neill, Paul. *The Oldest City: The Story of St. John's, Newfoundland.* Ontario: Porcepic Press, 1975, p. 59.

Lysaght, A.M. *Joseph Banks in Newfoundland & Labrador, 1766: His Diary, Manuscripts and Collections.* Berkeley and Los Angeles: University of California Press, 1971, p. 144.

Millais, J.G. *Newfoundland and Its Untrodden Ways.* New York: Arno Press, 1967, p. 5.

Thomas, Aaron. *The Newfoundland Journal of Aaron Thomas 1794.* Edited by Jean M. Murray. Longman's Canada Limited, 1968, p. 171.

"In the Very Early Days of Settlement." *The Newfoundland Character: An Anthology of Newfoundland & Labrador Writings.* Edited by D.W.S. Ryan and T.P. Rossiter. St. John's: Jesperson Press, 1984, p. 112.

Buchan, Captain David. *Captain David Buchan in Newfoundland.* Edited by Bernard D. Fardy. St. John's: Harry Cuff Publications Ltd., 1983, p. 37.

Noble, Rev. Louis L. *After Icebergs with a Painter: Summer Voyage to Labrador and around Newfoundland.* London: Sampson, Low, Son & Co., New York: D. Appleton & Co., 1861, p. 198.

Gwyn, Richard. *Smallwood: the unlikely revolutionary.* Toronto, Montreal: McClelland and Stewart Limited, 1968, p. 297.

Thomas, Aaron. *The Newfoundland Journal of Aaron Thomas 1794.* Edited by Jean M. Murray. Longman's Canada Limited, 1968, p. 118.

Power, Gregory J. *The Power of the Pen: writings of Gregory J. Power.* Selected and edited by Harold Horwood. St. John's: Harry Cuff Publications Ltd., 1989, pp. 22-3.

O'Neill, Paul. *The Oldest City: The Story of St. John's, Newfoundland.* Ontario: Porcepic Press, 1975.

Old-Time Songs and Poetry of Newfoundland. Gerald S. Doyle Limited, 1966.

Froude, Capt. John W. *On the High Seas: The Diary of Capt. John W. Froude Twillingate -1863 - 1939.* St. John's: Jesperson Press, 1983, p. 136.

Froude, Capt. John W. *On the High Seas: The Diary of Capt. John W. Froude Twillingate -1863 - 1939.* St. John's: Jesperson Press, 1983, p. 98.

Thomas, Aaron. *The Newfoundland Journal of Aaron Thomas 1794.* Edited by Jean M. Murray. Longman's Canada Limited, 1968, p. 53.

Millais, J.G. *Newfoundland and Its Untrodden Ways.* New York: Arno Press, 1967, p. 6.

Index